Polar

Polar

Dobby Gibson

ALICE JAMES BOOKS

FARMINGTON, MAINE

10 9 8 7 6 5 4 3 2 1

Alice James Books are published by Alice James Poetry
Cooperative, Inc., an affiliate of the University of
Maine at Farmington.

Alice James Books
238 Main Street
Farmington, ME 04938

www.alicejamesbooks.org

Library of Congress Cataloging-in-Publication Data
Gibson, Dobby, 1970-
Polar : poems / by Dobby Gibson.
p. cm.
ISBN 1-882295-49-8 (pbk.)
I. Title.
PS3607.I266P65 2005
811'.54--dc22
2004028195

Alice James Book gratefully acknowledges support from
the University of Maine at Farmington and the National
Endowment for the Arts. ❦

Contents

❄

❄

Acknowledgements

I am grateful to the editors of the following publications in which some of these poems first appeared in slightly different forms:

City Pages:	"Upon the Pillsbury Poppin' Fresh Doughboy's First Visit to Mill Ruins Park, Minneapolis"
Conduit:	"Flying Buttress," "From Whose Youth It Now Slowly Moves," "Under Erasure"
Crazyhorse:	"Recidivism"
Fence:	"Upon Discovering My Entire Solution to the Attainment of Immortality Erased From the Blackboard Except the Word 'Save'"
Forklift, Ohio:	"Aqua Velva," "Destiny Mannifesto"
The Iowa Review:	"Polar"
New England Review:	"What You Should Think About Doing Instead"
Octopus:	"Open Season," "Gone Before"
Ploughshares:	"No Surrender"
Third Coast:	"Ballistics Report," "Bee Sting Memories," "Chiropractic"
Slope:	"Kinetiscope," "Long Fence Sunrise," "Receiving Line"
Swerve:	"Outphysicaled," "From This Year's Indispensable Guide for Every One of Us"

Several of these poems also appeared in the *Fuori I* and *Fuori II* anthologies. I am grateful for a fellowship from the McKnight Foundation, which aided in the completion of this book.

Not this without: my family and friends, especially the Oversight Committee of Dean Young, Cornelia Nixon, James D'Agostino, and Karen Carcia. The Gooch. Matt Hart. Sam Prekop and the Sea and Cake. Pavement. And Kathy. Kathy. Kathy.

Polar

Like the last light
spring snowfall
that seems to arrive
from out of nowhere
and not land, exactly, anyplace,
so too do the syllables of thought
dissolve silently into the solitude
of the body in thought.
Like touching your skin,
or the first time I touched ice
and learned it was really water
and that neither were glass,
so does the jet contrail overhead
zip something closed in us,
perhaps any notion of the bluer.
Glancing sunlight,
my shoulders bearing the burden
or any theory why these birds
remain so devoted
to their own vanishing.
One store promises flowers
for all your needs,
another tells you
everything must go.
One river runs like a wound
that will never heal,
one snow falls like a medicine
that will never salve,
you the Earth, me the moon,
a subject moved in a direction
you desire, but for reasons
I believe to be my own.

Long Fence Sunrise

First there was a horrible storm
followed shortly thereafter by a horrible storm,
and when ultimately we emerged
from our homes only old couches slouched
there half buried in snowmelt
beneath a redundant dramaturgy of late morning sun.
We the otherwise nude had been inside,
pleading with one another,
laughing, using our tongues,
then dazed on our own front stoops
by the day's blank announcement:
winter is dying.
The traffic reports finally broadcast
what they meant to say all along,
"Stay the hell home,"
so we soon fled to the kind
of place a lonesome tractor
might sputter out halfway
though a field and cover itself
in a turtleneck of rust,
forcing all who pass
to measure from a distance
the cosmic American puzzle:
beauty half about the showboat dying,
half about the weird hay bales
too big for every known mouth.
We had been on all fours,
praying, coupling mightily,
searching for lost buttons.
There was a horrible storm,
then another we knew to be quelled
the moment the next hurled
some newer precipitation at our feet.
There were many storms,

a few that we chased.
There was the sound of banjos
picking hellfire bluegrass,
then the sound of banjos
never to be played again.

Gone Before

Sadness, though your beard may be fake
your anonymity is quite real,
whispered the dying man to his nurse,
raising his arms for his last sponge bath.
Early renderings had no vanishing point.
Painters dream in oil. Dreams, like canaries,
are sent down into our mineshafts
to discover how long we might survive;
the dreamers, like secretaries,
are sent home in sneakers, carrying their pumps.
Sadness, you are so Japanese: snow
on just one side of the leaf
that has not yet dropped.
Snow of all snow and of every lost chance,
last insects walking in fear across glass,
zeppelin beacons pulsing through the fog.
Snow as illegible as the cardboard
held by the man who can't spell
how hungry he is,
kneeling frozen at the fountain
to sail a small boat
folded from his last dollar.
Seen from deep orbit, cities wink white with loneliness.
A mother pulls her daughter by her arm.
A little girl pulls her doll by its hair.
Inside the space capsule after splashdown:
no one. And not even a note.
The hospitals they have built
just for people like us to die in
are built entirely of corridors,
which they keep empty,
except for a grinding light.
Outside, the snow falls without making a sound.
And still the dogs scatter.

Open Season

1.

It may be true that everything
has already been said,
but it's just as true that not everyone
has had a chance to say it.
A man walks into a bar.
The sunlight lies in measured lengths.
The afternoon stares right through you
in disbelief like the secretary
who you know never liked you,
as if forever waking from a dream
and being unhinged by the realer thing:
sometimes you, sometimes her, always this world
in which rock n' roll is dying yet another death
in front of children who will realize
only after it's too late,
then spend the rest of their lives
pretending it turned out otherwise.
You can explain such things
best by demonstrating
how they should never be done,
as if every life were lived in a second language,
hoping one another out of our mistakes
and toward another meal
even as we stare into the bathroom mirror
to rehearse the day's lies,
just as the face of every astronaut best records
the reflection of his own photographer,
more surprised than anyone
to find himself there,
standing on the moon.

2.

If everything has already been said,
then few appear to have been listening.
There isn't any part of "no"

that we have ever understood.
A hint of the invalidity, perhaps,
but only in a blousy kind of way,
radio dreaming in static,
mothers pushing strollers
through the heat in a sadness
we have yet to invent a greeting card for.
Light teaching us
what we never seem to learn:
a sparrow on the fencepost
and then just rain there,
no more bugs dying in our wine.
What of this surprise of sunlessness
is the souvenir that we leave with?
To look is to bear how close
we have come to being overcome—
by these stars, charted as if they were ours,
one day running into another
like two friends who can't admit
how much they can't stand one another's wife.
Beneath the alien cloud-wander,
murmurous inclinations, thoughts quickly brushed off
like the ash from your pants
at a party you prayed never to end,
floodlights unexpectedly low,
fluttering in tandem
in the very square they form,
as captive to the passage
as they are undefeated by night.

3.

It's true that at this time of year
it's already been said that it's all downhill from here.
One needn't hang around long to discern
the manner in which a steady inattention
to the hum can melt
into a thrumming kind of somnolence,
but we've drafted entire evacuation plans

for lesser emergencies than these,
and the directions still fail us.
As if just some trees could ever be enough,
when we're left here,
among our friends, already missing them,
hoping for what we know
won't be around for long:
flowers, or even just the smell of them.

Destiny Manifesto

What little I have to say
about the seizure of opportunity
is that it should be taken,
and quite seriously at that,
because it's one thing
to have the last laugh,
quite another to be the first to stop—
it depends what's blowing in off the lake.
A convergence of birds, perhaps,
thriving in collective disobedience
as if to affirm a capacity for a new order.
Their spells secret, and so wanted,
the clouds scattered to broken,
the sands now traveling through
the bathing suit of a beautiful woman
like a galaxy barely comprehensible
spinning within a universe
never to be understood,
a dust of light fluttering
among immeasurable matter
like a weaponless army
marching by torchlight
born silent in the heart of little speech.
Every day the papers are filled
with such stories: bodies betrayed
by thoughts of the body,
taggers bombing trains,
something fractured and ancestral
washed up along the shore.
Yet regardless of whether one loves,
or loving, whom, in this warm rain,
now pooling fuel in vacant streets
as a train rumbles across a bridge,
as one drives under that same bridge,
under the influence,
under the suspicion that God,

in order to create this world,
had to make Himself much smaller
than anyone suspects,
smaller than that which rises on the horizon,
distant and immutable,
a failed architecture nonetheless
hailed for lying west of the old.

Aqua Velva

Try waiting for a bus
while simultaneously looking away
from its expected arrival
and you'll see what I mean
about drawing curtains
on the pandemonium of the noble struggle
in the theater of the eye.
Dress blown back against a body
to reveal a body.
A body once revealed, discovered,
once discovered never forgotten.
A body blown back across the street,
in front of the travel agency window
that lists the cities you will never see
next to all the different amounts of money
you will never have,
and so have surrendered to,
like the world's most sensitive thief
pulling a revolver on the sea
and demanding nothing,
or the Japanese rock garden the Western eye
no longer mistakes to be simply rock.
There is a riddle to this river
that asks us to spend our whole lives here,
bleeding into it.
In the breeze. In the crossing. Blown back.
It is one thing to sing unto
the lovely thusly,
quite another to have her sing unto you.
Just imagine it,
in the evening, fleets of underthings
manned and then abandoned by wives.

What You Should Think About Doing Instead

Make sandwiches of pesto
and square luncheon meats.
Fear poison-arrow frogs. Fidget. Fall.
Live Tuesday in an iron lung.
Decipher the inscription of sad dogs
along the world's tallest totem pole.
There was a man in Iowa
who hiccupped for sixty-nine years.
There was an Indian with thirty-inch fingernails,
a left hand of brittle snakes.
Give it music. Angular rhythms. Rapid yodeling.
Soon you add voices,
then dense, thick harmony.
Dress it all in a gown of generous streams
beneath the hiss of dusk.
Mail your stamp collection.
Don't worry, the wine is tight,
but it will loosen up.
For now chew thoughtfully on your glasses.
For now watch the u and e
line up like quiet Londoners in queue.
I'll speak in tongues and it will go much faster.
As soon as afternoon fractures,
we'll both hear the drums more clearly, get zozzled.
Forget about the places you'd rather not be:
Walla Walla, Cucamonga, Timbuktu.
This is Vegas, where the machinery weeps quarters.
This is the combination to the safe
behind the velvet painting.
This is an island where waterfalls
drool all over themselves,
where bees step into blossoms
and mine tiny morsels of gold.
Everywhere are cats or else small animals
wearing fantastic pants.
This is Scotland where Mel Ednie

made the books with a twelve-pound onion.
Notice the bears as they awaken.
Don't be afraid, they're plastic and full of honey.
It's still the popular subject of all time: love.
But not the paired imitation kind.
Or the kind where she
eventually showers with your friend.
Forget the stray hair recovered,
the unseen moment it leapt
from scalp to sweater, snapping tether.
Think about that man with the beard of bees,
the one so fat he was buried in a piano crate.
No known human language
is without the vowel a,
and no funeral is without its music,
its laden rhythm of shoveled earth.
Consider the Siamese twins
and their reported sex lives,
the woman so tiny she worked as a king's doll.
Someplace far from here a guru
strolls over smoldering coals.
Much closer is the child in boots
afraid to strike a match.
In Baltimore, science grows human ears
on the backs of mice.
Everywhere we play the roles
of characters dressed exactly
as ourselves, though unconvincingly.
Full chorus now: Have mercy on us.
Now we can straddle the baroque.
Now we can set the record straight.
Eventually yesterday fades, or she fades,
and finally even love,
and what's left is not the comet,
all fire and pulse, but its smear
of slowly melting diamonds.
Play this again now that you know all the words.

Amateur's Night

How now small the casual present
appears from back over the shoulders
of its own, long shadows,
proving, at last, tree to mean tree,
me to mean world, darkness grief,
if only for an instant, like a return to a time
when one could pass through life with fewer things.
Life is mostly dreamt—just ask around.
Only this much sleeplessness
can have no possibilities beyond
its ceaseless needs and distances,
the night as we'll never see it,
a single, perpetual night,
creeping in sequence slowly
though the cities of the world,
melting another beauty right through her curtains
like the language within this language
that disappears after registering some small part of it.
Everything this moment has been brought
to you by: this sense of shame,
which has been brought to you by this rain,
which has been brought to you by these clouds,
which are made from the cast-off vapor of bird dreams.
Satellites carry the voices of young brides
screaming at their wedding planners.
Poisonous rumors seep from deep inside the funeral homes.
Thanks to the invention of the trailer,
expensive boats follow us wherever we go.
We lie awake, beneath the stars,
as unamazed as Chinese acrobats
beneath their constellations of spun plates.
In our chests, hearts don't beat.
We're given a number and told to get in line.
The papers report we're short on nurses.
The nurses whisper we're long on wounds.

Upon Discovering My Entire Solution to the Attainment of Immortality Erased From the Blackboard Except the Word 'Save'

If you have seen the snow
somewhere slowly fall
on a bicycle,
then you understand
all beauty will be lost,
and how even that loss
can be beautiful.
And if you have looked
at a winter garden
and seen not a winter garden
but a meditation on shape,
then you know why
this season is not
known for its words,
the cold too much
about the slowing of matter,
not enough about the making of it.
So you are blessed
to forget this way:
a jump rope in the ice melt,
a mitten that has lost its hand,
a sun that shines
as if it doesn't mean it.
And if in another season
you see a beautiful woman
use her bare hands
to smooth wrinkles
from her expensive dress
for the sake of dignity,
but in so doing trace
the outlines of her thighs,
then you will remember

surprise assumes a space
that has first been forgotten,
especially here, where we
rarely speak of it,
where we walk out onto the roofs
of frozen lakes
simply because we're stunned
we really can.

Upon the Pillsbury Poppin' Fresh Doughboy's First Visit to Mill Ruins Park, Minneapolis

Always this body, though never its consequence,
the light, which appears open and, therefore, impossible.

Dogs stumbling into us in their tenderness.
Like all the people we walked past today

and said nothing to, and the way all of it was ignored
by the tiny cameras—millionaires

sipping spritzers in their condos, medieval limestone,
the ghosts of flour dust, laughter exhaled like air

from a slashed tire. Memory is the one word
we have for this, memory of a sweetness in a dream

that was the world as we thought we knew it,
disappearing in a fire that was never named.

Who would have thought the new order we created
to destroy the old order would now live among us

as yet another birthright? Everything about the end
had been rehearsed in advance, even the ribbons they let us cut

merely for reaching it. One river bank staring at another,
barges slipping downstream at a speed

mysteriously slower than the river's own. A strangeness
still soft in the middle, still desperate for touch.

From This Year's Indispensable Guide
for Every One of Us

Last night I dreamt
I wasn't dreaming.
I dreamt I wasn't even sleeping,

and when I finally did close my eyes
I saw the dead
as they see us now,

stunned and unknowable,
old shirts left hung in the yard
among the skittish prophesies

of small birds.
Sleep can be like that,
a young man lying in a coffin

he built for himself,
imagining the sea
when he feels only his lightness

and how long has he lain there?
To you there is no hour
to retreat before, and so no answer

that is not also false.
But there is something that you need,
and there is a beautiful woman

leaning into the lillies
to describe just exactly
how she feels.

From Behind the Backward Neon Open

If not for suspecting
you were still on the floor
weeping into the neck

of the dog, then perhaps
I might have stayed here longer
and returned with more

of what this dreadfully
dim-lit November night
has me squandering.

Something about the last cars
ghosting home from work
steady behind headlights

appears shyfully sane
to those left not so.
The last autumn wind

dutifully delivers its itinerary
of further weathers,
but it's only another

brand of shuddering.
The bus is late.
You, still in your coat.

The brake lights
flickering bloodshot,
red at the stop sign, then gone.

From Whose Youth It Now Slowly Moves

What if the very desire he has been mailing
glances to finally did leave the lipstick
behind in the weathered vinyl of that booth?

What if his every notion of love
couldn't flag a cab? In her brisk stomp
and behatted disappointment

with the cold, unforgiving boulevard
there surely would be some promise.
Perhaps then he could stretch out

an open palm, offer something
practiced in that movied voice:
"You are a mysterious attic whose trembling rafters

know not the songbirds who seek their shelter."
It must make him feel suddenly old,
quickly conscious of the world's way of rooming him

amid these restaurants of dense paneling.
What was he finally hoping to see?
It's a question whose leap toward

a routine and whirring need
falls as unnoticed as the extension cord
behind this radiator, that booth.

Pipes hissing electoral promises.
Echoes in the seltzer.
Only now can he believe it: the shadows cast

by the petals of that silk rose
onto the petals of that same silk rose
suggest a new and far lovelier bloom.

Under Erasure

Take this for the eye, not the tear,
the once and again,
the apparent night
as it advances something,
anything about the living who,
missing their wings, despair.
Some slunk in shame,
leaving as they do, love almost so,
diaries of twilight cast into the fire.
Take this, and then this,
some pain to become realer,
perfumes from a profounder sleep,
moonlight puddling at a sudden cant.
Whisper heavy to these sins,
absolute clarity, second homes,
madmen practicing their falconry.
No miracle beyond the parade,
every undoing enacted in its brassy passing.
What isn't a last request?
First test the water with your finger.
Then test your finger with her mouth.

Solstice

I.

If the sun truly is our beginning and the moon
the first of the great many silent

movie endings, then this has to be about
letting one's guard down so that we

are finally allowed to see ourselves include
ourselves among the others in a hiatus of enmity.

Nothing less than holding out for the more
we couldn't have asked for, some sign

in suffering, some in knowing the weather
by what happens to our hair.

Anything for a smile. And so the clouds gather
like the last bridal party upon the lawn,

true again, it's raining, it's pouring,
the kids are spitting from the bridge.

II.

Of the distance, let us enlist the necessary
time. Of the time, best to refuse

what is at first shown. In between,
crooked in the night, lightning

striates the sky, hinting only
at the miraculousness of a newer sky.

Amid the delirium of the abating illusion,
the intractable pattern resembles

nostalgia less than it does commemoration.
In the connecting nightscape,

in the permissiveness of the imagined,
just beyond the beginning, the very where

the memory was first born and then burned
onto the backs of our eyes.

III.

Useless to me any concern
over what holiday next might befall this place

where what snow falls throws out backs,
where darkness is used only to fill

our empty parking lots with sorrow. Of the wind,
nothing defines its shape save for the landscape

it is not, yet destroys, confessing its crime
solely through recommission. Of the landscape,

nothing defines its shape save for the streetlights
powered by the river we dare to drink.

If we are not alone we think mostly as if,
and if we are not cold we are forecasted

soon to be, forever partly-something,
forever mostly-something if not soon completely.

IV.

Small snow, but falling quickly and in
quantities to constitute a substantial burial.

Snow of chanced limitation,
in which passion is as futile

as rations are old fashioned. Love blank.
Measured in absence. Paradise reduced

to the glaring light of its obliteration.
There is no taking anything back

in these additional dimensions now added
white to the amnesia of our own arrival

among the newly defined components of moments.
Whatever this kingdom of silence requires

of us, we have little choice but to assure
one another we imagined precisely this.

V.

This has gone on long enough.
Or at least most will read it that way,

half notes lost in the draperies
of the past or passing anticipation

of ascent, funerary in its rehearsed
associations for the bored cloister.

Now, after yet another seasonal evocation
by yours truly, the racket finally shifts,

falls to its knees, beseeches you.
Any breath is just as stubborn,

a long spilling, an untasted fruit,
the glistening handiwork of a life half spent,

so grateful for the sameness, even after crossing
the river simply to sip from another shore.

VI.

From the other side, shadows without circumstance
joust among the phony scenery like wallpaper

for swimmers. In our dreams, the poem
is seen only through this solution,

reluctantly possible at best.
Eddies of dismantling survived by a drawing

hope that meant something once.
Each page: what it wouldn't give.

Each perversely yours in sculptured bafflement
and the rhapsodized hysteria of eras gone by.

Over the falls in a barrel: an experiment
worthy of the falling waters

of the end beginning and the descent
into the torrents of reformation.

VII.

This kind of cold can only be about
this kind of slowing,

flakes to the ground like the bleached ash
from a fire that still burns

in a dead man's dream.
In it, every voice is essential, essentially

unabsorbable in the freeze of this neighborhood
of irrelevant reflections. Who would have guessed

our lives could be so much our own
in a world where only poets dream of poetry?

Where no space can be left long empty
from the approaching spill, or even its rumor.

Where sorrow is forever measured
and then overcome by distance.

VIII.

The secret is out and as delicate
as the skin along the wrist

of a young woman learning piano.
Despair is caked into the footsteps

of consolation like a useless fossil.
The city is calling us every name

in the book if at all from behind
its anonymous precincts of office-tower glass.

A lost-letter marquee of forgotten films
crooked in the corners of the mind.

Diviner planets like the future flicked apart
into its few known particulars,

destination rising in speech as unprovoked
as it is delivered to the silences of the indifferent.

IX.

Getting carried away. Neither shown
nor told, but a new way, a third way,

in this world only to refuse this world.
The robot of twilight grins fiendishly

as if made flesh. Calculus of self-absorption.
Imitates art. Isn't fair.

Moviegoers, sashed in the actual,
snoop through the pain of every particular.

Winter as if nothing has ever happened.
Each false thing petty in the slush

of the shabby and young, the puppies of junk.
So many selves enduring the circadian darkness

descending without sound outside and into
the joy of the convertible of surviving.

X.

Absent here by choice but suggested
unavoidably like the silhouette

never truly concealed from how one feels
learning another thing it ain't over till,

another irrelevant melting because temporary.
Shadows of passersby like tantrums thrown

in public and all over the sidewalk.
The art of art in arbitration:

these days, this is progress.
And among us, only poets here,

reading as if wrestling will teach us the body,
as if cripplingly lost in that place in the book

that is not a book where we all pause
to pay our respects to the misunderstandings.

XI.

Commuting to and from the world
held in the past and how it came to be,

the longing still transparent under the implants,
the poison sucked from the wound

by first freshening the wound. We can see
the future if it surrounds us,

we can relax one another arguing
the history of light. Eclipsed to see,

invested in the darkness for a glimpse
of the nametag, shocked to discover

business there, among the humdrum,
in the experimental theater of memory that cares

in one's stead, waiting on the corner
of the conversation, unable to speak.

XII.

The snowflakes taxi. The full moon
coolly punctuates the fantastic, howls the ohs

of its own vowels. Firemen stop for directions.
Children light cigarettes and wish

they had invented their own feelings.
The explorers who discovered only oceans

we cannot name. In the distant universe
there are things older than the light

that illuminates the firmament, a place where every
thought is a kind of unmarked car,

where women wait inside the revolving door
with a spritz of perfume and a secret

for the lonlier side of ourselves
we recognize only in what little it will admit.

XIII.

The light trembles, like a breath in the cold.
Another revelation of solitude

we can look upon, finally, with pleasure.
The complicated elegant, the simple cardinal,

sudden blood drop in the snow.
As if simply to say, "This survives."

But upon whose shoulders does the simple sit,
the silence, even the future singing,

"It is not possible for the bird
to speak back to the greatness of poetry!"

Red and white. Feathers on ice.
Carefully the words of a line, abstract purest

in the heart unsymbolic. I'll tell you
why this is beautiful: it's already being forgotten.

Chiropractic

I'll only admit what I have to:
like all disappointments
this begins and ends with the remembrance
of what it once was
not to have to face it,
before itself soon vanishing,
passive-aggressively buzzing me off,
like that roommate who never gave
me my phone messages.
To put it another way,
is this supposed to be weather or furniture?
Who could help but wonder,
the snow spattering hoods,
snapping wipers, and so heavy
I would swear it to be made of anything
but spit and angels' lust.
Behind my head, immaculate clouds gossip
over the equal and opposite forces
unaccounted for: the lone spindle of a sloop
centering the bay, a body desperate
for just such a measure
of what I hoped to see all along.
And then what I hoped never to see
on the inkblot test: animal splatter
rotting on the interstate,
felled lamp pole, shattered dome
of bug-encrusted glass,
and still the relentlessly ambuscading light,
like one of those moons
surrounded by rings as if hurled
into the sky like a stone into a lake.
In updraft, flakes that are their own
best matadors melt into headlights
in dazzling self-destructions
performed solely for me,
like watching a waiter deliver a cake

to the sea. A lost flake
grazes the sulking mouth.
A chip in the goblet
and so it isn't red wine
running from my lips after all.
You'd know it just by the look on my face:
gawking up into the first
finally rescuing orange torque
of afternoon sun strobing
through a spire of oak branches
gilded thinner than the sense of hope
pervading the man selling balloons
across the boulevard there,
so near the funeral.

A Presentation to the Gods Who Lack a Palace

In what had been until now merely morning,
indebted solely to the dawn,
business casual bleaching its retreat,
an invisible hand bewildered with pleasure.
Whereof the brightness had eyes,
ears for prayers, spirits raised in glass,
mirroring all we presumed to transcend:
the immeasurable means of exchange,
the body-to-body, sheathed in silence,
softest light pregnant with storm.
Among the stones, the memory of water.
Underwater, the memory of rain.
Now, in the rain, the desire to douse
the fires that savage the obscure.
Between towers and sleep, murmuring reliefs,
hymns for tired wretches,
sirens casting light among shadows casting suspicions.
From pummeled concrete,
crossbeams, scattered sheaves,
ash waiting to be blessed. Cranes salvaging in the rain.
Many are the worships that come to this,
the dreams of the fearful, in which the past settles nothing.

False Negative

It begins with the misunderstanding
that what you're being told
is being delivered
by what you're staring at,
the lips of the trusted
wrapped around a vocabulary
you've lived with forever,
now unable to wake up
the same person
you fell asleep as,
now looking back incredulously
at the one who holds you.
Impossible and so somehow more real,
here where you never wanted to be,
this light in the face
so desperate to speak, as if to say,
"This is where it emanates from."
The voice that departs
as another arrives,
both saying precisely the same thing
about the feeling you've
been here before,
the feeling of a familiar feeling,
carrying around someone
who looks exactly like you,
pulling off the same routine
in the tired office
of another American evening.
Words meaning two things at once,
so what is least
central to performance
becomes its primary subject,
like the endless knocking
that rises from
the suitcase at your feet.
It will begin,

with contrast and distraction,
an architecture of echoes
in the abstractions of wood,
like any art made
by obliterating its very tools,
the way setting
fire to a guitar
became the instrument's
most famous solo.
It's already begun,
and already gone are the times
when we would have believed otherwise.
Just as what you've been waiting
longest to hear is often said
by the one you don't believe
you see speaking,
which is easy for you to say,
you're not the one
with another's hand
around your heart.

Bee Sting Memories

I don't believe in God
was written all over the elastic waistbands
of that weather's wandering laundry
as it razzed what was left of us,
still loitering, still swapping dares.
What else was there to do beneath a sun
that made such a lousy dartboard
for a few planes thrown errantly
through this heckling rec room of ours?
It was a kind of game,
but so was anything
that involved unfolding a map,
funny money, and a die so multi-sided
that once thrown, never stopped
tabulating your potential.
We called it Mother.
As usual, most quit.
Some were called to supper.
The rest agreed: no pool towel
could ever be big enough.
But no matter how often
we spoke of them,
trapped in windows,
drowned in potato salad,
there was still that mysterious flower work.
The eyelash radar. Honey on a corn muffin.
And at that hour, evening doing its kabuki,
lifeguards shocking the pool,
no one could have foreseen such an advance.
Across the trawling lawns,
the terraced leeway, they flew in spite
of what we knew:
where it dangled in the doorway
behind the clotheslined strike zone
of the steel realty sign
that marked a house

being either constructed
or meticulously torn down.
Suddenly there was a neighborhood of wounds
hissing for salve, split bike tires, heat lightning.
I remember a chandelier
papered in venom.
I remember a book
about a pirate named Jim
and everything about that air conditioning.
I remember being told to sleep, go to sleep,
they're now far away,
crash landing in distant fields,
lying shoulder to shoulder
to die in black and white
like schoolbook soldiers.

Shepherd's Pie

Tonight the nation's most-ridiculed lunch lady
sits in front of this bar's Tabernacle Choir of liquor bottles
to drink a beer while still wearing her wet rubber gloves.

Overhead, the ceiling fans that landlord her dreamscape
spin tales of the jukebox's unappreciated bass players,
still haunting Midwestern hockey rinks, still nodding along
to the rock anthems in which they only ever half-believed.

This is the bar where she drafts her annual letter to *Sports Illustrated*,
canceling her subscription after receiving the Swimsuit Issue,
because this is a place she can turn away from the world
while still feeling it stare back, like a battalion of mimes.

Tonight, for the first time, the former shoe salesman
whom she will one day marry, divorce, and then share custody
of the dogs, sits on the stool next to her.

He leaves tomorrow to work on the ice harvest.

She thinks: He has the million-dollar smile
of white yachts parked in a midnight marina.
He thinks: Blondes don't do anything for me
that brunettes haven't been doing for years.

"My motorcycle has five speeds," he says.
His glass of beer sends a billion bubbles to the surface
like a pack of rehabilitated balloons released back into the wild.
"Six speeds if you include stop."

Everything he thinks of her he holds in his head as delicately
as he once held the heel of his loveliest customer.

She says, "The Chinese say that once you save a life,
you're responsible for it forever." Her heart beats
with the rhythm of a car passing with a nail in its tire.

He says, "A lie is just the truth plus something else."

She reaches out and touches him where his medal of valor once hung.

"I wish," he says, "you didn't have to wear those gloves."

Encroachment

To those who say time
conquers all philosophy,
I wonder what you make of this
and the reasons long dreamed of,
but like our reflections,
always one step too late.
It is November again.
The leaves are falling,
and then, as if that weren't enough,
the rain is, too.
True to its mission,
the cold makes us feel old.
Over what we were
and never finally are.
What we saved, or hoped for,
what we found and whom we never will.
Rain on my skylight.
Rain by any other name.
And like any prayer
it seems to hold out hope,
like the books we always had our heads in
while still pretending otherwise,
swearing to ourselves
that if we ever did find
a way out of this we'd never ask
for anything again,
content to be these prematurely old souls,
ordering out of habit,
unable to recall what any
should finally be remembered for:
their bread, or way with the truth,
or even this very air, like greater breathing,
right here, speaking of autumn nights
as if filled with a new voice
larger than our own.

Receiving Line

Despite what those religions think,
steeples aren't that much closer to God,
though surely He would rather the occasional cross
jab into the nape of His floofy mattress
than all these phone poles,
arranged as they are in such an obvious worship
of one another, like athletes.
Probably for even the slowest atheists
this week has been track and field,
a vault slo-mo over an enormous precipice of thaw:
it's luncheon-meat cold, and even winter rain
isn't anything new, but it hurls itself
at us like a smashed chandelier,
pocks the lawn's snow into a kind of tapioca
and now, suddenly, is it groceries we're after?
And if not artichoke, what to name this yearning,
the one that sends us to the street with so many keys?
The produce of desire is thusly bagged
separately where its functions are misunderstood
and subatomic like hockey.
Shadows fall dumbly to the pavement
like bored skydivers,
deciphered quickly like the tiny books
sold near the register, and just out of sight,
a drawer full of mittens unpaired,
abandoned umbrellas, tremendous galoshes,
a rare form of beauty independent of
its frame that the otherwise blistered long ago
hysterically sings in its historical garden.
We all wonder how a single wire
holds simultaneous conversations,
what it is here that seems to have fallen
from its shelf, or if that's precisely the point:
among the shelfless, the struggle of the putting-back
is that none know where to start.
On the one hand, the rules were thrown out,
on the other, so much more is expected of us.

Recidivism

Best to remember that aside from lunch,
so much is already decided,
cleaved and planed beneath long ago's glacier.
We must finish our weary skiffle.
The avenue's flickered light
can only gather in the leaves.
We have no say in the day's drunken tincture,
or in the hiss of this beer's fizzle.
There are just tiny choices:
when to slake thirst,
how to part the mug's foam,
what to think about the way
you once brushed her cheek with yours
so that you both flushed, if only slightly.
Ignore the murmur of voices
from adjacent bedrooms
as they rise like memory's steam.
For now, unzip your partite, sarcous self
and tune the radio,
swig dry sherry behind the wheel.
Drive past the factory that smells of melted candy
as those around you rapidly merge.
Soon you may crave a long danish in Eau Claire;
eventually you may crave an éclair in Denmark.
To understand the heart, you must first move
away from home and then back
as you carefully mimic the blood.
Most bumper stickers will translate
as "I'm better than you,"
all graffiti as "I did this."
If only it weren't so difficult after hello,
the words as difficult to catch as fish shadows,
everywhere the sound of bones
as they knit, blood as it clots.
Everywhere are squirrels who swallow,
swallows who can't, fish without eyelids.

What kind of way is that to go through life,
trapped inside death's muddled stare?
Feet once dangled in the deep end
and it was then a matter of when
to reach for her lips,
but also when you'd be handed your knapsack
on some morning's corner.
If it's not desire, it's hope,
which often leaves us fumbling
in prayer behind the wheel of a Datsun,
trying to piece together
one severed fabric or another.
Soon you'll return to the offices of small verdicts,
the overhead gunshot of shoes.
The lobby escalators as they rise
slightly toward the heavens.
And the side to the escalator few ever see:
the steps as they fold into themselves,
as they return to do it over again.

Kinetiscope

It's impossible to make
much hope out of all this ruined foliage,
out of anything people
already have too much of,
plastic bags sopped black at the curbside.
So the first thing you do
is try not to,
trying to remember a time
before it was like this,
forced to publicly swallow your own warfare.
Outside there is a leaf
that has stained the sidewalk
the color of a bruise.
It's what the morning's mapped, electrical
zodiac could never have forecasted:
while we were longing for these leaves,
the leaves were longing for these trees.
And the trees, now leafless,
checking us into our little motels
of despair, just stand there
combing skies soon to bring snows
already elsewhere in rehearsals of plummet.
They say it may have been
the last thing you ate,
the last where you breathed,
though even science guesses.
There isn't anything that couldn't end
this violently: what you were about to say
to your dinner guest, beloved, self.
And it wasn't until the moment you were sure
it was jailing you in a kind of forever
that you learned all is long past
and they're once again blessing you for creating
what you secretly tried to destroy.

Outphysicaled

So smallish our sense of weather
heavy here beneath this thin innuendo of June,
still too soon, and how the despondent,
in this light, no longer seem quite so.
So smallish our sense of too soon
that hardly summers, and when it does,
will be too late. Late enough for St. Paul
to once again X its calendar
of open windows, any way to commemorate
all of this going, going, now as gone
as the last absence, sixth sense
no better than the third,
because no matter what the pencil marks
on the doorjamb once measured
of the neighborhood girls,
it will always be apples to oranges,
guns to butter, as anything we might
finally have put a name to
some god has long since imagined a shape for,
which just goes to show you:
what the valets pull to the curb with a wink
is typically that in which we never arrived,
like yesterday's parked car
that seemed to hold nothing
but the protruding bareness
of a woman sunning
her absurdly long legs
through the open passenger window,
uncrossed and then crossed again
at the naked ankle,
with toenails painted
as if all had eyes to see them
and none had hearts as red to bleed.

Flying Buttress

I.
More attention should be paid to the dramatic
pauses. This first snow as softly as snow
can happen, sky sniffling, like a child
in a laundromat, miserable autumn socks
stained with regret. Chicago prone,
desperate for even a sloppy autopsy
of sun, every solitary mortuary
curtain drawn. Because these clouds lead
nowhere but to themselves: from lion

B.
to Oldsmobile to lion. An enormous casserole
of fallen angels, the tiptoes of the dead
and their empty butterfly nets above a planet
of hands in search of puppets.
Now there are over 7,000 reasons
to cough, a storm in the Specific Ocean
the untrained forecast as a flushing drain,
a spun bun, a flung pudding—
it's all in the timing now that the jokes

3.
are read from cards. And this is what we thought
we wanted, until nothing appeared
in the mirror but this: a shivering breast, a sock
on a foot that was just a sock,
until worn on a hand, and now he's named Oscar.
He says he's cold and awfully thirsty.
How easily the bed of that pick-up received
those hurled bottles. How quickly the snow
puts all that smashed glass to sleep.

Ballistics Report

I shall not seek, nor will I accept
                    the loose and unkempt strands of autumn
          now tightly wound into winter's starch
                              like hair into a turban. What survives
          is no such thing worthy of this
silence, a lake bored solid,
          trees swearing wooden oaths,
                              Chicago surviving on just the idea
of mountains, a theory of oceans.
          Upon further questioning, lilacs,
                    did you or did you not bloom, and where
          were you the night of the first
                    flake's glance and its unique reminder
of gravity? Back, and to the left.
Back, and to the left. There's too much
          of this going around and yet none
          remember with what they've been charged,
                    who they hoped would hurl rose
                              petals from the balcony, surprised
the defense has chosen to rest.
          Fellow Americans, have you ordinary
                    and indispensable desired the secret
taken with, here again, and now
                    less heartening by half? Repeat after me:
          I, too, without being sure.
But what is hope if not evolution established,
                              a tiny stool stored in a locker,
the opportunity of a neighbor's
                    couch left out by the curb, a thought
on the other hand. It's a philosophy
          of cages: a man invented a shutter so quick
          you saw a shot bullet exit an apple
                              and ever since then it's been
a matter of playing within yourself.
          No matter how many boats may pass,
                    you still fight the instinct to wave.

No Surrender

Now that my poetry is finished
and I'm once again grateful
for what passes as real
in this version of my life, my favorite one,
the one in which, in late evening,
the lake appears
to hold another, more beautiful sky,
never again will any time
so quietly pass.
These perceptions soon lost,
if only because everyone's first wish
has always been to see
himself through another's eyes.
By merely looking we make casts
of these shadows, the ones that forever
point back to ourselves
by mimicking the very holes
we punch in the moonlight,
mugging for the camera,
chatting about this and that
even as the bird flies
into the glass door and dies.
There is a precision to absurdity
that illuminates the immeasurability of the truth,
and we'll never know one another
more intimately than when we share
precisely these kinds of misunderstandings.
Place your hand on my shoulder.
Empty your pockets into mine.
Now you've caught your thief.

Great Plain

There is at first
so little here exposed.
There is falling
on our heads: rain,
sequential and hunting.
Nightfall, so spottily noticed,
makes its way chromatically
across the lawn.
Whether to eat out or in,
words from their tongues,
witnesses with disposable contacts.
Behind closed doors,
the geniuses of the world
pissing again in the shower.
There's a different set of lips
for every kind of suggestion.
It was at first thought
that one's first thought
was one's worst thought.
This since has been rethought,
and now, amid this larger
sorting out, we search
for a more final shade
to this extenuating gray,
rain zombifying us with its symmetries,
stripped of our musics,
each to ourselves
in a dark and silent corner.
There are things and names for things.
And names for the things
that are happening to things:
decorated, consumed, forgotten.
Hands for other thoughts,
hands for handling,
for passing along the declarations
that mark each day's paper

as a new edition,
flipped so casually as they are
into the neighborhood at dawn.
We weren't invited,
but we were asked to wait,
and in what time passes
for someone's idea of progress,
a billion Chinese fall
in and out of love
and there's a star
in the sky for every one
of them and for every one
of us to wish upon.
Amid the middleness,
there's the feeling
that anything can be seen
but nothing reached.
Like language called a joke
because it returns only our gaze,
there is a vigilance in belonging
out of a feeling of betrayal.
One way to think of it
is mishearing the lyrics,
another is making a new song.

* * *

So all at once night
and staggering be the long day,
seemingly without us
or any warning,
maybe a little familiar,
still nothing we
would ever stop for, or save.
Not even for what's both
lost and possible,
soon snow gardens,
veins of randomness,

last autumn light cast unused
into a summer porch.
The deep lawns,
mumbling to their hearts,
which they hold in their laps
as they lie under these trees
beneath a kingdom of silences
we'd rather not face.
To the weather here
we assign our cold,
to the principle, the contrary,
to the hour this late already,
or the idea of houses
built primarily for women
to bathe in.
Two hands for undressing,
one mouth for lies,
a moment for every question
we save only for ourselves,
like that one about how
we can stand it here,
or how the fog can sink,
as if it knew
we were no longer looking,
wondering what happens to a shadow
forced to fall inside another.
Radiant burial, late-known night,
rain and the echoes
of falling rain.
Lost dog, glad witness,
deepening our trance,
moon as moon,
passion as a way out,
one to another,
the lost as they were found,
the look of this place
and the one on her face
that we'll never forget.

* * *

Here's how our river sings it:
There isn't anything
I can't divide in two
or hurl into the sea.
What we had for dinner,
what we used to grow it,
the sense of pride we felt
believing it was all ours.
The song is called swallowing
and the instrument is the act itself,
erasures poured into a past
by a rain that isn't new
to any of it,
the innocent role-playing,
the rescue fantasies,
the mail still warm from the box,
demanding money.
The almosts prove too much,
almost pure, almost impossible,
smashed into useless shards
like the vase we couldn't let them take,
no matter how much
we wanted them to leave.
Now there's light rain,
later there's a chance
of light rain.
Now there's that look
in our eyes:
we find it cold.
It's what has made us
masterful negotiators.
For insofar as an attention
to the evening's gloom
can make us say something
back to ourselves,
such dull light becomes the rock

upon which the past is scuppered.
Every fossil into fuel,
this wind into tears,
the reason why
the wrecked look innocent
but cannot forgive.

* * *

Beneath a sky
made of the parts
of a forgotten sky
we turn to one another
as if without history.
The first bird appears ecstatic,
says, "Take me home."
A bike rack's double
cast by the streetlight
in fierce geometries
across the snow—
soon always snow,
this coffee still worth a chance.
Last sparrows,
whom we will not mourn,
surrender quietly in a way
that we have no verb for,
and so are as tragic or joyous
as we want them to be.
We haven't lived long enough
to know any of this for sure.
The river moves
with or without us,
full of unused seeds,
old tires, bodies.
Last leaves from the sugar maple
as it rises into a frost
falling delicately as a realization
that we're not the kind of people

we thought, at this age, we would be.
Leaves and the shadows
of fallen leaves.
Last roses. Last light dying
in the sky, red
that is not a rose.

* * *

None of it feels new, of course,
or should we say newer,
fumbling through squash
at the market in search of
that next something slightly better
we swear we're worth.
Brought down to the level
of our everyday sentences,
the clarity of the contest
renders us spectators.
So we bid farewell to the festival.
So long to its imminence.
Like a great shadow
thrown in front of an inexpectant eye,
eventually even rest comes to rest,
night water heavy
with its farewells, its cancellings.
An absence made for arrivings,
though we who dare return
will never quite know what lies beneath.
Looking back at the beginning,
we should acknowledge
that it does have a memory after all.
It has left a wound,
if no wounded.
Most of it had yet to register,
like our sense of direction,
or that laugh we used to have.
We lost them,

and we're at a loss to explain why.
These two coasts—
can we call them that?—
grinding at one another over
everything we'll never know,
like one of those arguments
years after which we realize
both of us were right.
In creating its own form
it's always perfect,
validating its one great idea
with every feathery pulsing,
living in a present
comprised entirely of its past.
The light bulbs are bare
and they've painted the walls white
as if to prove it.
The sign lit red above the door
spells the one word
we all understand to be
our only means of escape.
Outside, incoherence is said
to melt away in the shy lamplight,
though a man has to be
far poorer to abandon
what he sees.
We kneel at the water,
but it's too busy
to show us what we
most wanted to see,
the wondering, turning our backs
on the moon
beneath bare trees.

     *   *   *

And the river,
which reflects back to us

only the poisonous yellow
lights that illuminate the bridge
we built to cross it.
When we look to the sky,
we look to the oldest light,
so we can travel back in time,
just not very far.
Truth such as this
is as surprising
as it is disappointing,
as it is forgotten,
quickly, like rain that falls
onto the pavement like dying angels.
From here, panes of glass
frame the stars tenderly
in a darkness they cannot illuminate.
Hope, nearly mad and then the last look
lifted from what tonight
stumbles into song.
Somewhere, contented in their harbors,
the beautiful feel weightless
by the sea.
It's sworn to be the truth
on this side of the river,
maybe even on the other,
or by the river itself.
So we take to the avenue,
leaving our umbrellas behind,
thinking our heads will do.

Recent Titles from Alice James Books

Pennyweight Windows: New & Selected Poems, Donald Revell
Matadora, Sarah Gambito
In the Ghost-House Acquainted, Kevin Goodan
The Devotion Field, Claudia Keelan
Into Perfect Spheres Such Holes Are Pierced, Catherine Barnett
Goest, Cole Swensen
Night of a Thousand Blossoms, Frank X. Gaspar
Mister Goodbye Easter Island, Jon Woodward
The Devil's Garden, Adrian Matejka
The Wind, Master Cherry, the Wind, Larissa Szporluk
North True South Bright, Dan Beachy-Quick
My Mojave, Donald Revell
Granted, Mary Szybist
Sails the Wind Left Behind, Alessandra Lynch
Sea Gate, Jocelyn Emerson
An Ordinary Day, Xue Di
The Captain Lands in Paradise, Sarah Manguso
Ladder Music, Ellen Doré Watson
Self and Simulacra, Liz Waldner
Live Feed, Tom Thompson
The Chime, Cort Day
Utopic, Claudia Keelan
Pity the Bathtub Its Forced Embrace of the Human Form, Matthea Harvey
Isthmus, Alice Jones
The Arrival of the Future, B.H. Fairchild
The Kingdom of the Subjunctive, Suzanne Wise
Camera Lyrica, Amy Newman
How I Got Lost So Close to Home, Amy Dryansky
Zero Gravity, Eric Gamalinda
Fire & Flower, Laura Kasischke
The Groundnote, Janet Kaplan
An Ark of Sorts, Celia Gilbert
The Way Out, Lisa Sewell
The Art of the Lathe, B.H. Fairchild
Generation, Sharon Kraus
Journey Fruit, Kinereth Gensler

Alice James Books has been publishing exclusively poetry since 1973. One of the few presses in the country that is run collectively, the cooperative selects manuscripts for publication through both regional and national annual competitions. New regional authors become active members of the cooperative, participating in the editorial decisions of the press. The press, which historically has placed an emphasis on publishing women poets, was named for Alice James, sister of William and Henry, whose fine journal and gift for writing went unrecognized within her lifetime.

Typeset and Designed by Dede Cummings
Printed by Thomson-Shore

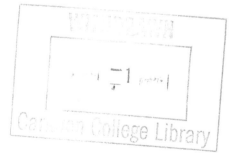